TRUE
LOVE
WAITS

TRUE LOVE WAITS

COMPILED BY

MARK DEVRIES

BROADMAN
& HOLMAN
PUBLISHERS

Nashville, Tennessee

© 1997
by Broadman & Holman Publishers
All rights reserved
Printed in the United States of America

4263-52
0-8054-6352-6

Published by Broadman & Holman Publishers, Nashville, Tennessee
Acquisitions and Development Editor: Janis Whipple
Page Design: Anderson Thomas Design

Dewey Decimal Classification: 241.66
Subject Heading: SEXUAL ABSTINENCE/YOUTH—SEXUAL BEHAVIOR
Library of Congress Card Catalog Number: 97-8903

Unless otherwise noted, Scripture quotations are from the Holy Bible, New International Version, copyright © 1973, 1978, 1984 by International Bible Society. Other versions cited are KJV; NASB, the New American Standard Bible, © the Lockman Foundation, 1960, 1962, 1963, 1968, 1971, 1972, 1973, 1975, 1977; used by permission; and The Message, the New Testament in Contemporary English, © 1993 by Eugene H. Peterson, published by NavPress, Colorado Springs, Colo.

Library of Congress Cataloging-in-Publication Data
True love waits / [compiled by] Mark DeVries.
    p.   cm.
    Summary: Presents excerpts from the "True Love Waits Bible"—Scripture verses,
quotations, survey results, and more—offering guidance on setting limits on sexual
behavior.
  ISBN 0-8054-6352-6 (pbk.)
    1. Teenagers—Religious life. 2. Chastity—Quotations, maxims, etc. 3. Sexual ethics
for teenagers—Quotations, maxims, etc. [1. Sexual ethics. 2. Sexual abstinence. 3.
Youth—Sexual behavior. 4. Christian life.] I. DeVries, Mark.
BV4531.2.T78   1997
241'.66—dc21

                                                      97-8903
                                                       CIP

            1 2 3 4 5   01 00 99 98 97

FOREWORD
················

It was at our honeymoon hideaway cabin deep in the mountains that I learned for certain that true love really does wait.

When my new bride came to bed and my arms encircled her, I knew that we were both sharing this experience for the very first time. Sure, I had cared for other girls before, but there was a part of me that I had saved for her alone. And even when she was a Football Sweetheart and had all the dates she wanted, she and God had decided—before she'd ever laid eyes on me—that she would share with me what she had never shared before.

They say that God has the best sex planned for those who wait. And you know what? "They" were right, and it's catching on. True Love Waits has been covered by hundreds of media outlets, including "48 Hours," "20/20," "The Today Show," "Nightline," CNN, "Oprah," "Donahue," "TheSally Jesse Raphael Show," "Leeza," MTV, *Newsweek, Time, Life, Mademoiselle, Seventeen, Teen, Vogue, Glamour, USA Weekend Magazine, Rolling Stone, Details, Sassy, Playboy, USA Today, The New York Times, The Washington Post* (front page), *The Washington Times* (front page), and *Associated Press.*

If you make the True Love Waits promise to God, you will not be alone. You'll be joining hands with hundreds of thousands of other teenagers around the world who have become a part of a counter-cultural revolution. You wouldn't believe how many adults have been completely caught off guard by teenagers who choose purity as a lifestyle.

The very fact that you are holding this book means you are at least considering choosing God's best. On each page of this little book, you'll read one more reason why true love really does wait. Some of the studies may surprise you. Some things may shock you. You may hear ideas you've never heard before. But the bottom line is that you won't have to make this incredibly important decision alone. You'll find in these pages examples and experts, folks much like you, giving you reasons to remember...

...true love really does wait.

Richard Ross
Spokesperson
True Love Waits

HAVE YOU TAKEN THE PLEDGE?

Believing that true love waits, I make a commitment to God, myself, my family, my friends, my future mate, and my future children to be sexually abstinent from this day until the day I enter a biblical marriage relationship.

–500,000+ teenagers around the world

Love is patient.
1 Corinthians 13:4

SOMETIMES SEX SOUNDS A LOT LIKE LOVE...

"I want you" doesn't mean
  "I want to give my life to you."

"I need you" isn't the same as
  "I will be here for you."

"You're gorgeous" doesn't mean
  "I love you for who you are."

"Look how happy we are" isn't the same as
  "I will be content with you 50 years
  from now."

Don't be deceived.
James 1:16

"It feels good" doesn't mean
   "I want you to feel good about yourself
   when it's all over."

"I'll be gentle" isn't the same as
   "I care about your feelings."

"Everybody's doing it" doesn't mean
   "I want us to do it God's way."

"It's so good, I want it now" isn't the same as
   "It's so good, I'm willing to wait for it."

Sex is not the same as love
   no matter how similar they sound.

–Ruth Senter, *Campus Life Magazine*

> *Love does not delight in evil but rejoices with the truth. It always protects, always trusts, always hopes, always perseveres.*
> *1 Corinthians 13:6-7*

TRUST THE INVENTOR

> The man and his wife were both naked, and they felt no shame.
> Genesis 2:25

Overall, sex is not a big subject in the Bible. Other topics—particularly our relationship to God—take precedence. When the Bible does discuss sex, however, it reflects exactly the attitude you'd expect from an inventor writing about his invention. The Inventor, better than anyone else, appreciates what His invention means. He's happy to speak of it. He understands how it works and knows exactly what it's good for. He doesn't overload you with instructions, but cuts to the heart of the subject. He tells you how to put His invention to practical use.

The Inventor is very firm about His ideas. He doesn't spend a lot of energy explaining why things are the way they are. He just insists: this is the way it works!

The Bible's view of sex can be put very simply: Sex is wonderful within marriage. Outside marriage, it's an offense to the Inventor.

–Tim Stafford, *Worth the Wait*

So God created man in his own image, in the image of God he created him; male and female he created them. God blessed them and said to them, "Be fruitful and increase in number...." God saw all that he had made, and it was very good.
Genesis 1:27-28, 31

WHY AM I STILL SO LONELY?

The most sexually active single people are usually the loneliest....sex feels intimate, but since it can be a substitute for intimacy, it does not satisfy for long.

—P. Roger Hillerstrom,
   Intimate Deception

"Why spend money on what is not bread, and your labor on what does not satisfy? Listen, listen to me, and eat what is good, and your soul will delight in the richest of fare." Isaiah 55:2

Some of our first conscious experiences back in baby-hood make it seem as though Mom and Dad's main responsibility is to keep us from having fun. One of my first memories was of having my hand slapped for trying to stick a fingernail file into an electrical outlet. Why would these cruel giants resort to physical punishment just to keep me from experiencing the joy of putting this object into the hole it was obviously made to fit? At the time, it seemed like they were simply trying to destroy my fun. I had never enjoyed the thrill of 110 volts coursing through my tiny body. Why would they deny me such an experience?

–Ken Davis, *How to Live with Your Parents without Losing Your Mind*

WHY WOULD GOD SAY "NO"?

As a father has compassion on his children, so the Lord has compassion on those who fear him.
Psalm 103:13

The Greek word "porneia" (from which we get the English "pornography") is the most common New Testament word used to describe sexual activity that is "out of bounds" from God's perspective. The word occurs nine times and is most commonly translated as "sexual immorality" and sometimes as "fornication" ("human intercourse other than between a man and his wife")…. The Bible's consistent condemnation of sexual immorality affirms undeniably that there are certain expressions of love that God designed exclusively for married couples.

Mark DeVries, *True Love Waits Bible* ⋯⋯⋯

DOES THE BIBLE EVER REALLY SAY IT?

Flee fornication. Every sin that a man doeth is without the body; but he that committeth fornication sinneth against his own body.

1 Corinthians 6:18, *KJV*

THE BOTTOM LINE

Chastity is the most unpopular of the Christian virtues. There is no getting away from it: The old Christian rule is, "Either marriage, with complete faithfulness to your partner, or else total abstinence."

–C. S. Lewis, *Mere Christianity*

The body is not for immorality, but for the Lord, and the Lord for the body. 1 Corinthians 6:13

ALL BY YOURSELF?

A survey of teen leaders across the country—those listed in *Who's Who Among American High School Students*—showed that:

- 59% are nondrinkers
- 57% attend religious services weekly or more often
- 82% don't use drugs
- 73% are virgins

—Lane Powell, *The Dating Book*

Therefore, since we are surrounded by such a great cloud of witnesses, let us throw off everything that hinders and the sin that so easily entangles, and let us run with perseverance the race marked out for us. Let us fix our eyes on Jesus. Hebrews 12:1-2

AGAINST THE FLOW

Even a dead fish can flow with the current; it takes strength to swim against it.

For the grace of God that brings salvation has appeared to all men. It teaches us to say "No" to ungodliness and worldly passions, and to live self-controlled, upright and godly lives in this present age. Titus 2:11-12

WHEN IT'S ALL OVER

The degree of heartbreak when a relationship ends is directly affected by the degree of physical intimacy shared in the relationship.... You can't put a condom on your heart. Our outside conduct affects our inside condition.

–Robbie Castleman, *True Love*

Above all else, guard your heart, for it is the wellspring of life. Proverbs 4:23

There's another slightly goofy aspect to this. People...suggest it's because Christians are so sexually repressed they want to make everybody else just as miserable as they supposedly are: "Christians just aren't happy as long as someone, somewhere, is having a good time."

But where exactly is this party that Christians want to spoil? Some individuals are having fun, but a lot of people are having a miserable time. You can't cut the statistics to read any other way. Millions of divorces, adulteries, and abortions add up to something other than fun.

–Tim Stafford, *Worth the Wait*

WHERE'S THE PARTY?

But the fruit of the Spirit is love, joy, peace, patience, kindness, goodness, faithfulness, gentleness and self-control. Against such things there is no law.
Galatians 5:22-23

The kind of treatment we receive is directly related to how cheaply we sell ourselves or what kind of treatment we hold out for....The point is clear: Once we give ourselves away cheaply, we will not experience the treatment that is equal to what we are worth.

–Rick Stedman, *Pure Joy*

You will be a crown of splendor in the LORD's hand, a royal diadem in the hand of your God. No longer will they call you Deserted, or name your land Desolate. Isaiah 62:3-4

Sexual experiences do not reinforce a person's ultimate value and importance. Singles who give themselves sexually feel depreciated, marked-down in price....No longer are they treated like prime rib; now they are just meat loaf under generic catsup.

–Rick Stedman, *Pure Joy*

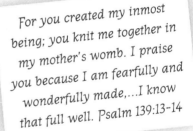

For you created my inmost being; you knit me together in my mother's womb. I praise you because I am fearfully and wonderfully made,....I know that full well. Psalm 139:13-14

MEAT LOAF?

Many people compare sex to Play-Doh... [it] doesn't require much sophistication to use at maximum efficiency. It's just fun.... If you're marketing Play-Doh, the main thing is distribution. Get it out to as many people as possible, and let them make up their own rules as to how to use it.

On the other hand, marketing dynamite is quite different. You have to be careful about who buys it, and you have to encourage the buyer to use it carefully.... You can move mountains with dynamite, but you also can blow yourself to pieces.

I think sex is more like dynamite than Play-Doh.

–Tim Stafford, *Why Wait For Marriage?*

JUST PLAYING WITH PLAY-DOH?

Do not offer the parts of your body to sin, as instruments of wickedness, but rather offer yourselves to God, as those who have been brought from death to life; and offer the parts of your body to him as instruments of righteousness. Romans 6:13

THE COST OF LOVE

Love is not something you catch, like the flu. Love is like a garden. It grows slowly and takes a lot of care and nurturing. Real love, genuine love, God's kind of love is going to cost you time, time and more time.

–Dawson McAllister,
How to Know If You're Really in Love

If real love was just the feeling of being wildly attracted to someone, why do more than 50 percent of teenage marriages wind up in divorce? Could it be that they confuse something else for love?

–Mark DeVries

> "Enter through the narrow gate. For wide is the gate and broad is the road that leads to destruction, and many enter through it."
> Matthew 7:13

THE NEW REVOLUTION

First, they questioned marriage. Said that love should be "free." But "free love" turned out costly—very costly for some. Now, they're... saying sex should be "safe."

But "safe sex" can be risky (to your health and your heart).

"If you hold to my teaching, you are really my disciples. Then you will know the truth, and the truth will set you free." John 8:31-32

We think it's time for a new revolution. We think it's time for a love that is real...and lasting...and pure. A love that sees sex as a celebration of two lives shared together. Forever.

That's why we believe in marriage. And we're saving sex for it.

Bob Bowne: Law Student
David Dettoni: Youth Worker
Yvonne Duvier: Actress, Singer
Caroline Metherell: College Student
Dana Glover: Musician, Model
Rob Anderson: Medical Technician

–Family Research Council poster,
Used by permission

Marriage should be honored by all, and the marriage bed kept pure. Hebrews 13:4

MAYBE IT'S TIME FOR A CHANGE

WHY SO DISAPPOINTED?

I talked to twelve teenage girls about their first sexual experiences. Ten used some form of the word "disappointment" in their descriptions.

Exhorted by the media, their peers, their boyfriends, and subtly encouraged by their parents who are afraid to discourage, teenage girls are having their sexual initiations earlier than their mothers did. And not enjoying it more. The revolution hasn't freed them. It has, in fact, exploited them.

There is a way that seems right to a man, but in the end it leads to death. Proverbs 16:25

"At least it didn't hurt as much as I thought it would. It wasn't fun either. Now that's all he wants to do. I'm sorry I started, but how do you quit?" (Melissa, age 16)

"My first time was right after we saw *Endless Love* on cable TV. We were alone at his house. We had some wine. I thought it was going to be wonderful, like in the movie. I was really disappointed." (Carol Ann, age 15)

–Susan Crain Bakos,
   King Features Syndicate

IN THEIR OWN WORDS

Do you not know that your body is a temple of the Holy Spirit, who is in you, whom you have received from God? You are not your own; you were bought at a price. Therefore honor God with your body. 1 Corinthians 6:19-20

> Therefore shall a man leave his father and his mother, and shall cleave unto his wife: and they shall be one flesh. Genesis 2:24, KJV

AM I READY?

God has given a definite order for the use of His gift of sex: "Leave, cleave (be united), then become one flesh." If you're not ready to get married, you're not ready to have sex.

–Anonymous

When you've gone "all the way" together—or even most of the way—you may feel you are already essentially married and that a marriage ceremony merely ratifies what you've already done. So you may not think about the commitment as much as you ought to. But the fact is that the marriage ceremony is more than a ceremony. It takes you "all the way" into marriage. Sex doesn't.

–Tim Stafford, *Worth the Wait*

GOING ALL THE WAY

May you rejoice in the wife of your youth....may her breasts satisfy you always, may you ever be captivated by her love. Proverbs 5:18-19

THE COLD HARD FACTS ON MAXIMUM SEX

According to a recent Family Research Council Survey, the adults most likely to report that they are very satisfied with their current sex lives are those who are married and who strongly believe that sex outside of marriage is wrong.

–Gracie Hsu,
The Orange County Register Opinion

Humble yourselves, therefore, under God's mighty hand, that he may lift you up in due time.
1 Peter 5:6

WHEN THE FEELINGS FADE

Romantic love lasts
in its full intensity
for about 90 days.

–Robert Bella,
Rebuilding the Nest

Love...always perseveres.
1 Corinthians 13:6-7

IT'S MORE THAN YOU THINK

Sexual purity involves a lot more than simply being a virgin. Sexual purity is much more than not doing something....Purity isn't an act—it's a lifestyle.

–Susie Shellenberger,
Anybody Got a Clue About Guys?

And whatever you do, whether in word or deed, do it all in the name of the Lord Jesus, giving thanks to God the Father through him. Colossians 3:17

TECHNICAL VIRGINITY

> Abstain from all appearance of evil.
> 1 Thessalonians 5:22, KJV

I disagree with those who make virginity a technicality. Such people say that so long as two people don't actually have sexual intercourse they are all right. I say that God's concern for virginity is not a matter of anatomy but of privacy. He wants people to reserve some "private parts" for their marriage partner alone. Only in marriage ought two people to be naked and unashamed, as Adam and Eve were. When two people touch each other's sexual organs, I believe they are doing what is appropriate for married people alone.

—Tim Stafford, *Worth the Wait*

"Why shouldn't this be a popular option? Incidentally, a lot of people who came of age in the fifties went to the altar as virgins. Including me."

–Phil Donahue

LOOK WHO'S COMING OUT OF THE CLOSET....

For since the creation of the world God's invisible qualities—his eternal power and divine nature—have been clearly seen, being understood from what has been made, so that men are without excuse.
Romans 1:20

THE VOICE OF EXPERIENCE

My husband, Chris, and I dated for five years before we got married. It was hard, but we saved ourselves for each other. I know a lot of people don't; but speaking from the marriage side of the picture, it's definitely worth the wait.

–Terry Jones, Point of Grace

God intended for sex to be between two marriage partners—one man and one woman for the rest of their lives. Not only am I glad I waited because God commanded it, but also because I was able to give my husband a part of me that I had not shared with anyone else in the world.

–Jennifer Hendrix, Sierra

He who has clean hands and a pure heart,...he will receive blessing from the LORD....Such is the generation of those who seek him. Psalm 24:4-6

ARE YOU...

Too many people spend most of their time looking for the "right one." They ought to worry more about *becoming* the right one.

Let's talk specifics:

So whether you eat or drink or whatever you do, do it all for the glory of God.

1 Corinthians 10:31

Drinking and partying—People who get drunk, do drugs, and fool around in other ways make poor partners.

Studying—Surveys show that people who are willing to work to achieve good grades often make strong marriages because they are willing to work at achieving good relationships.

Faith—Those who have a strong faith in God and who live that faith out in practical ways (including such ordinary things as going to church), often have the stability and the idealism needed to make strong relationships.

—Tim Stafford, *Worth the Wait*

> He who walks with the wise grows wise, but a companion of fools suffers harm.
> Proverbs 13:20

THE RIGHT ONE?

HMMM...

Your beauty should not come from outward adornment, such as braided hair and the wearing of gold jewelry and fine clothes. Instead, it should be that of your inner self, the unfading beauty of a gentle and quiet spirit, which is of great worth in God's sight.

1 Peter 3:3-4

The front cover of the December 1990 issue of *Esquire Magazine* showed a beautiful picture of Michelle Pfeiffer with the story headline, "What Michelle Pfeiffer Needs..."

Most people would look at that cover and say, "Not a whole lot."

That's what made it so interesting when *Harper's Magazine* published the [following] bill that Esquire had received for the touch-up costs on Michelle's cover photo:

Date: 11 October 1990
Client: *Esquire*/T. Koppel
Product: December Cover/Michelle Pfeiffer
Description: Retouching 1 dye transfer two-piece strip of
Michelle Pfeiffer in red dress. Clean up complexion, soften
eye lines, soften smile line, add color to lips, trim chin,
remove neck lines, soften line under ear lobe, add highlights
to earrings, add blush to cheek, clean up neck line, remove
stray hair, remove hair strands on dress, adjust color and add
hair on top of head, add dress on side to create better line,
add dress on shoulder, clean up and smooth dress folds
under arm and create one seam image on right side.

Total: $1,525.00

–Duffy Robbins,
It's How You Play the Game

> The LORD does not look
> at the things man looks
> at. Man looks at the
> outward appearance,
> but the LORD looks at the
> heart. 1 Samuel 16:7

AND YOU WONDER WHY YOUR SCHOOL PICTURE DOESN'T DO YOU JUSTICE?

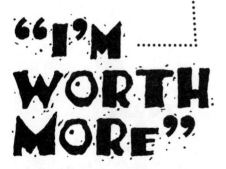

For the wisdom of the world is foolishness in God's sight.
1 Corinthians 3:19

"I'M WORTH MORE"

"By not giving into sexual desires when I'm involved with someone (which is getting more and more difficult), I realized I was telling my partner, myself, and God that I'm worth more than a cheap thrill or momentary gratification." (Jaclyn—22-year-old virgin)

–Rick Stedman, *Pure Joy*

IS THERE A PATTERN HERE?

Do not be misled: "Bad company corrupts good character."
1 Corinthians 15:33

A study published in *Pediatrics* magazine found that sexually active teens are far more likely than their celibate peers to be involved in a variety of self-destructive behaviors, including drug and alcohol use, school delinquency, and attempted suicide.

—Youthworker Update

ARE YOU READY?

Unfortunately, most people spend more time preparing to get a driver's license than preparing for marriage.

–P. Roger Hillerstrom,
 Intimate Deception

In a well-furnished kitchen there are not only crystal goblets and silver platters, but waste cans and compost buckets—some containers used to serve fine meals, others to take out the garbage. Become the kind of container God can use....Run away from infantile indulgence. Run after mature righteousness.
2 Timothy 2:20-22, The Message

HOW CAN I KNOW IF WE'RE REALLY COMMITTED?

Commit to the LORD
whatever you do,
and your plans
will succeed.
Proverbs 16:3

The wedding ceremony is our society's way of separating those with strong emotions from those with also strong commitment.

–Tim Stafford, *Worth the Wait*

Make no mistake: Making love doesn't make a person love you.

–Anonymous

MAYBE THIS WILL MAKE HIM LOVE ME

We must not be sexually promiscuous.
1 Corinthians 10:8a,
The Message

LUST...

is not noticing that a woman is sexually attractive. Lust is born when we turn a simple awareness into a preoccupied fantasy. When we invite sexual thoughts into our minds and nurture them, we have passed from simple awareness into lust. [Martin] Luther put it this way: "We cannot help it if birds fly over our heads. It is another thing if we invite them to build nests in our hair."

> Put to death, therefore, whatever belongs to your earthly nature: sexual immorality, impurity, lust, evil desires and greed, which is idolatry.
> Colossians 3:5

–Patrick Morley,
The Man in the Mirror

During premarital counseling my husband asks couples: "How long do you plan to stay married?" Everyone always says, "Forever." He responds with another question: "What do you know about love that makes you think your marriage will last when so many fail?"

–Robbie Castleman, *True Love*

POP QUIZ

Learning about love from TV is like learning self-defense from a Roadrunner cartoon.

–Tim Stafford, *Worth the Wait*

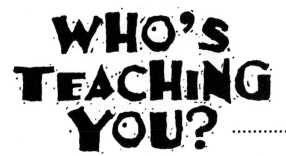

Dear children, do not let anyone lead you astray. 1 John 3:7

YOU KNOW IT'S TIME TO BREAK UP WHEN...

Jamie knew it was time to break up with Bo when...

- He kept calling her Marla;

- He insisted she change her hair color;

- He sent her a note addressed to Kelli;

- He always took the opposite side of everything she said;

- He never showed up on time and didn't bother calling to explain that he'd be late.

> Reckless words pierce like a sword, but the tongue of the wise brings healing.
> Proverbs 12:18

AND WHEN...

Mitch knew it was time to break up with Angie when...

• She kept "fixing" his hair;

• She always agreed with everything he said;

• She volunteered to do his laundry;

• She started becoming better friends with his parents than with him;

• She asked a million questions about his ex-girlfriends.

—Susie Shellenberger and Greg Johnson,
258 Great Dates While You Wait

"But seek first his kingdom and his righteousness, and all these things will be given to you as well."
Matthew 6:33

PRESSURE: THE WORST LINES AND THE BEST ANSWERS

Line: "Everybody's doing it!"
You: "That's not true. I'm not doing it, and tonight, neither are you!" (smile)

Line: "Nobody is going to care."
You: "Okay, let's go ask my dad."

–Greg Speck,
Sex: It's Worth Waiting For

Be strong and very courageous. Be careful to obey all the law my servant Moses gave you; do not turn from it to the right or to the left, that you may be successful wherever you go. Joshua 1:7

> "We want you to know, O king, that we will not serve your gods or worship the image of gold you have set up." Daniel 3:18

Line: We're going to get married. What difference does it make whether we make love before or after the ceremony?
Answer: Probably about the same difference it makes whether you practice medicine before or after you graduate from medical school.

Line: Don't worry, we'll stop before we go too far.
Answer: Don't worry, we already have.

—Tim Stafford,
 Worth the Wait

WHAT KIND OF MAN HAS THE MOST APPEAL TO WOMEN?

A survey of 30,000 women about their choice of husbands [revealed that] most of them said they had chosen their mates based on sex appeal, but 80% said that if they had to do it over again, they would choose a husband based on his ability to communicate.

–Josh McDowell, *Why Wait?*

> Pleasant words are a honeycomb, sweet to the soul and healing to the bones. Proverbs 16:24

"As the heavens are higher than the earth, so are my ways higher than your ways and my thoughts than your thoughts." Isaiah 55:9

THE PARTY'S OVER

More than 85% of boys who impregnate teenage girls will eventually abandon them.

–Josh McDowell, *Why Wait?*

HOW DO YOU SPELL CLUELESS?

> Therefore, I urge you, brothers, in view of God's mercy, to offer your bodies as living sacrifices, holy and pleasing to God—this is your spiritual act of worship. Romans 12:1

"I'm a junior in high school and captain of the football team. I have a girlfriend whom I like very much. Her name is Gwen. We have been going together for about seven months.

Lately, I've been getting a lot of pressure to have sex, but I don't think Gwen is ready. My buddies say something must be wrong with me not to have had sex with her yet. I sometimes feel like telling them to shut up, but what good would that do?

When I really think about it, the guys are right. I should start putting a little more pressure on Gwen to have sex with me." (Teenage student)

—Josh McDowell, *Why Wait?*

SCARY, ISN'T IT?

Ask around. You'll find out that most guys get a lot of their information about sex from other guys.

—Mark DeVries

Blessed is the man who does not walk in the counsel of the wicked or stand in the way of sinners or sit in the seat of mockers. Psalm 1:1

SURVEY SAYS!

More than 200,000 teenagers that were surveyed were asked what they thought about the following two statements:

When people find out that a boy has had sex, it hurts his reputation at school. 22% of boys agreed; 15% of girls agreed.

When people find out that a girl has had sex, it hurts her reputation at school. 70% of boys agreed; 87% of girls agreed.

—USA Weekend

A good name is more desirable than great riches; to be esteemed is better than silver or gold.
Proverbs 22:1

WHO'S LIVING A SHELTERED LIFE?

A silly idea is current that good people do not know what temptation means. This is an obvious lie. Only those who try to resist temptation know how strong it is....A man who gives in to temptation after five minutes simply does not know what it would have been like an hour later. That is why bad people, in one sense, know very little about badness. They have lived a sheltered life by always giving in.

—C. S. Lewis, *Mere Christianity*

> Do not love the world or anything in the world. If anyone loves the world, the love of the Father is not in him. For everything in the world—the cravings of the sinful man, the lust of his eyes and the boasting about what he has and does—comes not from the Father but from the world. 1 John 2:15-16

DOES EASY SEX MAKE MORE ROMANCE?

For every 18-29-year-old who believes life today is "more romantic" than forty years ago, there are four who think the exact opposite.

–William Mattox, *Family Research Council*

[Lover:] You are a garden locked up, my sister, my bride; you are spring enclosed, a sealed fountain. [Beloved:] ...Let my lover come into his garden and taste its choice fruits. Song of Songs 4:12, 16

WHY WAIT?

"I'll be able to say to my husband that I loved him before I even knew him and I decided to save myself for him."

–True Love Waits pledging teenager, *True Love Waits Bible*

This day I call heaven and earth as witnesses against you that I have set before you life and death, blessings and curses. Now choose life, so that you and your children may live.
Deuteronomy 30:19

> For such people are not serving our Lord Christ, but their own appetites. By smooth talk and flattery they deceive the minds of naive people.
>
> Romans 16:18

If love were just a feeling it would be easy. The alcoholic father believes he loves his family—on his own terms. While he has taken no responsibility for either babies or bills, he will sit in a bar and weep over how much he loves and misses his family. Love for him is a warm feeling and hot tears that demand no action.

—Kari Torjensen Malcom,
Building Your Family to Last

THAT LOVIN' FEELING

Love that is not expressed in action is not love.

–Ken Davis, *How to Live with Your Parents without Losing Your Mind*

Love has a bad habit of giving pop quizzes.

–Tim Kimmel,
Little House on the Freeway

"If you love me, you will obey what I command."
John 14:15

JUST DO IT

Those who are seriously attempting chastity are more conscious and soon know a great deal more about their own sexuality than anyone else....Virtue—even attempted virtue—brings light; indulgence brings fog.

—C. S. Lewis,
 Mere Christianity

But small is the gate and narrow the road that leads to life, and only a few find it. Matthew 7:14

Your feelings can trick you. The line between love and infatuation is thin. And frankly, sex confuses everything. To be physically involved clouds the issue. It makes you feel closer than you really are. It makes you feel as if you are actually in love. Maybe so. Maybe not.

–Jim Long, *Campus Life*

> *But each one is tempted when, by his own evil desire, he is dragged away and enticed. Then, after desire has conceived, it gives birth to sin; and sin, when it is full-grown, gives birth to death.*
> James 1:14-15

WANT TO BE CONFUSED?

> *Do you not know that your bodies are members of Christ himself? Shall I take the members of Christ and unite them with a prostitute? Never! 1 Corinthians 6:15*

IT'S NO BIG DEAL... (OR IS IT?)

The monstrosity of sexual intercourse outside marriage is that those who indulge in it are trying to isolate one kind of union (the sexual) from all the other kinds of union which were intended to go along with it and make up the total union. The Christian attitude does not mean that there is anything wrong about sexual pleasure, any more than about the pleasure of eating. It means that you must not isolate that pleasure and try to get it by itself, any more than you ought to try to get the pleasures of taste without swallowing and digesting, by chewing things and spitting them out again.

—C. S. Lewis, *Mere Christianity*

THE NEW CHASTITY

"For this reason a man will leave his father and mother and be united to his wife, and the two will become one flesh." Ephesians 5:31

Despite the Pill, legalized abortion, and economic freedom, our bodies are trying to tell us something: they don't necessarily want to be tossed around like lost luggage on a round-the-world plane trip....After close to two decades of sexual permissiveness...more and more young women are opting for the new chastity.

–Carolyn See, *Cosmopolitan*

For me, it's more than not wanting to get a girl pregnant or getting AIDS. It's about doing what's right. I believe that God created me and wants the best for me, and the best for me is to abstain from sex until I'm married.

–Jordan, age 19, *Abstinence; It Really Is Our Choice* (pamphlet)

So then, brothers, stand firm and hold to the teachings we passed on to you, whether by word of mouth or letter.
2 Thessalonians 2:15

WHY HE'S WAITING

IT'S JUST ONE LITTLE DECISION, ISN'T IT?

Every time you make a choice you are turning the central part of you, the part that chooses, into something a little different than what it was before. And taking your life as a whole, with all your innumerable choices, all your life long you are slowly turning the central thing either into a heavenly or into a hellish creature.

–C. S. Lewis, *Mere Christianity*

"Choose for yourselves this day whom you will serve....But as for me and my household, we will serve the LORD. Joshua 24:15

LOOKING FOR LOVE
(IN ALL THE RIGHT PLACES)

[My husband and I] didn't know that night how good we would be for each other. But the Lord did. Keeping our eyes on Jesus eventually gave us eyes for each other.

—Robbie Castleman, *True Love*

Delight yourself in the LORD and he will give you the desires of your heart. Psalm 37:4

Love:
Friendship
that has
caught fire.

–Anonymous

LEXICONARAMA

We loved you so much that we were delighted to share with you not only the gospel of God but our lives as well, because you had become so dear to us.
1 Thessalonians 2:8

DOES DATING REALLY WORK?

This is my lover, this is my friend. Song of Songs 5:16

It may be fun and exciting, but a steady schedule of plastic, programmed encounters is a poor way to detect character and an unrealistic way for young couples to prepare for marriage.

–Bill Hybels, *Fit to Be Tied*

THE LAW OF DIMINISHING RETURNS

> Flee the evil desires of youth, and pursue righteousness, faith, love and peace, along with those who call on the Lord out of a pure heart.
> 2 Timothy 2:22

Unless teenagers deliberately set limits on themselves, research has shown that within 300 hours of being together, a couple will have sex. Here's how that might compute: If a couple spends 13 hours per week together (two 4-hour dates and 5 hours at school), they will reach 300 hours in 23 weeks (less than 6 months).

–Dee Dee Stephens, *The Teen Advisors Notebook*

A wedding won't change a person from being self-centered to being sensitive and giving. If the person you're dating can't get along with his or her family now, a wedding will not create a different person for you.

–Anonymous

"By their fruit you will recognize them....A good tree cannot bear bad fruit, and a bad tree cannot bear good fruit."
Matthew 7:16, 18

MAYBE HE'LL CHANGE...?

I CAN SETTLE DOWN LATER...CAN'T I?

Can you really believe that people who've had a variety of come and go lovers, sex and all, are going to be able suddenly to turn around one day and believe single-mindedly in one love, committing themselves body and soul to building it forever?...I can't....Statistics bear me out. A variety of sources indicate that those who fool around before marriage have trouble after marriage.

As a dog returns to its vomit, so a fool repeats his folly.
Proverbs 26:11

–Tim Stafford, *Why Wait for Marriage?*

WILL YOUR LOVE LAST?

Sometimes it is hard to figure out whether a relationship is healthy and what areas need attention to keep it that way. With the relationship graph, you can quickly check the status of your dating relationship. It measures your intimacy in five crucial areas: emotional (feelings), physical (sexual), social (time together), intellectual (talking), and spiritual (sharing faith and life issues and experiences). The final bar on the graph is the level of commitment you and your partner have chosen.

"My command is this: Love each other as I have loved you."
John 15:12

Instructions: Taking one area at a time, do your best to determine how intimate your relationship is for each of the five areas by drawing a line somewhere between 0% intimacy and 100% intimacy. Then mark the level of commitment in the relationship. You may want to take the test twice—once for you and once for your partner, since you may come to the relationship with different levels of commitment.

TRY THIS TEST

	0	25	75	100
EMOTIONAL (the depth and intensity of your feelings)	0	25	75	100
PHYSICAL (your level of sexual intimacy)	0	25	75	100
SOCIAL (the amount of free time you spend with each other or on the phone together or doing something exclusively for each other)	0	25	75	100
INTELLECTUAL (the amount of time devoted to talking and communication)	0	25	75	100
SPIRITUAL (any communication about the deeper issues of life and faith, such as praying together, discussing how to live as a Christian, death, etc.)	0	25	75	100
DEGREE OF COMMITMENT (the level of chosen, deliberate, committed love in the relationship–100% being God's standard of marriage, engagement about 70% and so on)	0	25	75	100

The General Rule: If there are areas of the relationship that are beyond your willingness or ability to commit at this time, your relationship is likely headed for trouble.

"These things I have spoken to you, that My joy may be in you, and that your joy may be made full." John 15:11, NASB

–Chap Clark, *The Next Time I Fall in Love Journal*

EMOTiONS ARE FOR...

...feeling not for thinking. This may seem obvious, but my experience in counseling is that too many people call on their emotions to do critical thinking. This always leads to trouble because emotions are not equipped for those sorts of demands.

–Tim Kimmel,
  Little House on the Freeway

He who trusts in himself is a fool.
Proverbs 28:26

THE ONE SECRET EVERY GREAT LOVER KNOWS

Communication is...hard work.

When two people [on a date] can't find anything to say, they're tempted to fill the silence by getting physical. While making out does cover the embarrassment and even leaves a feeling of becoming closer, it never substitutes for communication. If you try to make it a substitute, you will wreck your relationship.

–Tim Stafford, *Worth the Wait*

> Let your conversation be always full of grace, seasoned with salt, so that you may know how to answer everyone. Colossians 4:6

WE'RE WHAT?!

What do pre-engagement "commitments" really mean? Whether you call it "going together," "going out," or "exclusively dating," you would be wise to know what kind of commitment you are making (and what kind of commitment is being given to you).

Make no mistake about it. Pre-engagement commitments mean nothing more than this: "I promise I will not date anyone else until I feel like changing my mind."

–Mark DeVries

> O magnify the LORD with me, and let us exalt His name together.
> Psalm 34:3, NASB

Put simply, you know it's getting too serious if you're starting to act married. That means that if you're progressing into married sexual territory, it's getting too serious. And if you can't make plans without consulting each other, it's getting too serious.

–Jim Hancock and Todd Temple, *Good Advice*

Dear children, let us not love with words or tongue but with actions and in truth.
1 John 3:18

GeTTing TOO SeRioUS?

A righteous man is cautious in friendship. Proverbs 12:26

IT'S TIME TO BREAK UP WHEN YOU SEE...

Forced Feelings—If you have to force yourself to get psyched-up about going out with someone;

Spiritual Straying—If the guy or girl you're dating isn't drawing you closer to Christ;

Handlin' the Heat—If you're being pressured sexually, emotionally, physically, socially;

Crowded Corners—If the guy or girl you're dating is calling too much, sending too many notes or, hanging around more than you're comfortable with;

Preoccupied Patterns—If you're sitting around waiting for the call, pretty much scheduling your day, your week, your life around this person;

Ouch! That Hurt!—If the person you're dating is constantly putting you down, criticizing you, or making you feel bad about yourself.

—Susie Shellenberger and Greg Johnson, *258 Great Dates While You Wait*

Having a good date life shouldn't be your top priority. Finding the person you will marry shouldn't be your top priority. Your top priority should be to love God and become more and more like Jesus Christ.

–Dawson McAllister,
  How to Know If You're Really in Love

Question: What is the chief end of man?
Answer: To glorify God and enjoy him forever.

–The Westminster Catechism

No eye has seen, no ear has heard, no mind has conceived what God has prepared for those who love him.
1 Corinthians 2:9

TOP PRIORITY

IS THIS THE ONE?

As a teen, I was friends with everyone, but I was extremely selective about whom I dated.

–Twila Paris

Do not be yoked together with unbelievers.
2 Corinthians 6:14

HOW FAR?

But among you there must not be even a hint of sexual immorality, or of any kind of impurity, or of greed, because these are improper for God's holy people. Ephesians 5:3

The reason physical affection between a guy and a girl is so exciting is because God designed it that way...and it's a progressive process—one stage naturally leads to the next....I don't believe most healthy Christians in a dating relationship, whatever their age, can progress much beyond [the casual kissing] line without asking for trouble. You need to realize that past this point you begin to arouse in each other desires that cannot be righteously fulfilled outside of marriage.

—Josh McDowell, *Love, Dad*

WHERE DO YOU DRAW THE LINE?

Several principles apply:

1. You should only do what is helpful for your relationship.
2. You should stay away from activities that create more frustration than appreciation.
3. Physical interactions shouldn't dominate the relationship.
4. You should keep private parts private.

–Tim Stafford, *Worth the Wait*

> But solid food is for the mature, who by constant use have trained themselves to distinguish good from evil.
> Hebrews 5:14

It's like driving 90 mph down a city street and a child runs out in front of the car. We may jam on the brakes and have every intention of stopping, but the actual decision was made when we chose to go 90 mph on a city street. Once that decision is made, it's sometimes very difficult to reverse. The same holds true in sexual temptation. The amount of physical contact and the setting a couple place themselves in are important factors in avoiding temptations. So the guidelines have to be drawn early enough so as not to get so excited and so involved sexually that they reach a point that it's difficult, if not impossible, to stop.

–Dwight Carlson, *Sex and the Single Christian*

A man's own folly ruins his life, yet, his heart rages against the LORD.
Proverbs 19:3

OUT OF CONTROL

NOW IS THE TIME

For chocoholics, Hershey, Pennsylvania, is not the place to decide whether or not to eat chocolate. Likewise, a party isn't the place to decide whether to drink or not to drink...and the back seat of a car isn't the place to decide how far you're going to go sexually....We can gain the courage to say "no" to a given activity if we start long before the situation calls for it.

–Brad Dyrness and Michael Ross,
 Just Say "No" but How?

> A prudent man sees danger and takes refuge, but the simple keep going and suffer for it.
> Proverbs 22:3

SUPPOSE YOU DON'T WANT TO BE KISSED....

For some folks, the answer is simple: "Just say so." But in case you're looking for something a little more subtle, try one of these tactics:

What Can You Say?

- "My lips are really sunburned."
- "I just had my braces tightened."
- "[Are] my parents...watching [again?]"
- "Have you ever burped and then began to taste the dinner you just ate?"

> Speaking the truth in love, we will in all things grow up into him who is the Head, that is Christ. Ephesians 4:15

<u>What Can You Do?</u>

- Clear your throat.
- Flip your retainer in and out of your mouth.
- Blow a [strategically timed] chewing gum bubble in the person's face.
- Let your dog out and give it a big slobbery kiss.

–Todd Temple and Doug Fields,
 Creative Dating

Your lips drop sweetness as the honeycomb, my bride; milk and honey are under your tongue.
Song of Songs 4:11

HOW ARE YOUR BRAKES?

A couple of weeks ago Andrea and I went on another adventure—this time on bicycles. She had just learned to keep her balance on a two-wheeler and was ready to leave the safety of the front street and try the hill behind our house. She'd never ridden down a hill before.

We sat atop the descent and looked down it. To her it was Everest. "You sure you want to try?" I asked.

"I think so," she gulped.

"Just put on your brakes when you want to stop. Don't forget your brakes."

"Okay."

I rode to the midway point and waited. Down she came. The bike began to pick up speed. The handlebars began to shake. Her eyes got big. Her pedals moved in a blur. As she raced past she screamed, "I can't remember how to stop pedaling!"

She crashed into the curb.

If you don't know how to stop, the result can be painful. True on bikes. True in life.

Do you remember how to stop?

—Max Lucado, *The Angels Were Silent*

How can a young man keep his way pure? By living according to your word. I have hidden your word in my heart that I might not sin against you. Psalm 119:9, 11

HOW FAR IS TOO FAR?

> That each of you should learn to control his own body in a way that is holy and honorable, not in passionate lust like the heathen who do not know God.
>
> 1 Thessalonians 4:4-5

In our culture, couples who have been going together for a while are likely to hug, kiss, and hold hands. I think these are, for most people, warm and innocent ways to express loving appreciation. When you go further and aim for sexual excitement, I think you generally stop speaking the language of love. Why? Because you have to stop somewhere short of intercourse. Some people can't—they lose control. Some people lose the desire to stop. Some people keep control, but they do so at the cost of feeling frustrated. Instead of feeling warm toward each other, they feel overheated. I have never known this to help a relationship grow, especially when people spend hours together revving up their motors and pushing the brakes at the same time.

–Tim Stafford, *Campus Life*

THE TOP TEN SEXUAL CON GAMES

"I am sending you out as sheep among wolves. Therefore be as shrewd as snakes and as innocent as doves." Matthew 10:16

Do not make friends with a hot-tempered man, do not associate with one easily angered, or you may learn his ways and get yourself ensnared. Proverbs 22:24-25

A con artist—especially a good one—is tough to spot. And sexual con artists can be some of the toughest to detect. Here are some of the most common tools used in a sexual con game. If you find a person you're dating using them, you may be the next victim.

1. Trust: "I can be trusted."
2. Secrecy: "And we can't tell anyone about us."
3. Jealousy: "I want his stuff out of your locker. Now!"
4. Insecurity: "I just really don't think I'm good enough for you."
5. Intimidation: "You'd better spill it now. I can find out!"
6. Accusations: "If you want him, just go out with him!"
7. Flattery: "You're smart, you're sweet, and you are very pretty."
8. Status: "There are a lot of other girls I could be going out with."
9. Bribery: "I'd buy you everything you wanted."
10. Control: "If I hear about it, you will have to deal with me!"

—*Unmasking Sexual Con Games,*
•••• Boys Town Student Guide

AND HE CALLED THIS LOVE?

In the course of time, Amnon son of David fell in love with Tamar, the beautiful sister of Absalom....He grabbed her and said, "Come to bed with me..."

"Don't, my brother!" she said to him. "Don't force me. Such a thing should not be done in Israel...." But he refused to listen to her, and since he was stronger than she, he raped her.

Then Amnon hated her with intense hatred. In fact, he hated her more than he had loved her. Amnon said to her, "Get up and get out!"

—2 Samuel 13:1, 11-12, 14-15

> [Love] is not rude, it is not self-seeking, it is not easily angered, it keeps no record of wrongs. Love does not delight in evil but rejoices with the truth.
>
> 1 Corinthians 13:5-6

DON'T BE CONFUSED

If you have been raped, molested or abused, as far as God's concerned, you're still a virgin. Your virginity is something you give away, not something that can be taken from you.

–Jacob Aranza

> The LORD is close to the brokenhearted and saves those who are crushed in spirit. Psalm 34:18

IF YOU ARE DEALING WITH ABUSE AND DON'T KNOW WHERE TO TURN, CALL 1-800-NEW-LIFE.

DATE RAPE: WHAT YOU NEED TO KNOW

Be wise about what is good, and innocent about what is evil.
Romans 16:19

Whether it's use of physical (grabbing, shoving) or verbal pressure, if this is sexual activity that you do not want, that you do not consent to, that you are pressured or forced into, it is rape—even if you know the guy, even if you have dated a long time—it is still rape.

Someone sitting or standing too close, who enjoys your discomfort; power stares—looking through you or down at you; someone who blocks your way; someone speaking in a way or acting as if he knows you more intimately than he does; someone who grabs or pushes you to get his way; someone who doesn't listen or disregards what you are saying (like when you say "NO").

—Campus Life Magazine

Love doesn't strut,
Doesn't have a swelled head,
Doesn't force itself on others,
Isn't always "me first,"
Doesn't fly off the handle.
1 Corinthians 13:5,
The Message

AND WATCH FOR THESE DANGER SIGNS

WHAT GIRLS THINK OF GUYS WHO LOOK AT PORN:

Lindsey: I'd rather not date a guy with a dirty mind, even if he's cuter than a guy with good values.

Amy: When I'm with a guy who treats me like a sex object, I want to go home. I want a guy with a clean mind. Are you out there somewhere?

> Finally, brothers, whatever is true, whatever is noble, whatever is right, whatever is pure, whatever is lovely, whatever is admirable—if anything is excellent or praiseworthy—think about such things. Philippians 4:8

Merritt: The thought of guys looking at pornography makes my stomach turn.

Liz: I wish guys could know how much it turns us off when they talk about porn. We lose a lot of respect for them.

–Lisa Kragerud, *Breakaway*

I will set before my eyes no vile thing.
Psalm 101:3

NOT A BAD QUESTION

Do I want my sex life to be incredible or bearable?

Have I consulted my most important sex organ (my mind)?

What is the point beyond which we create more frustration than love?

> See, I set before you today life and prosperity, death and destruction.
> Deuteronomy 30:15

> *Search me, O God, and know my heart; test me and know my anxious thoughts. See if there is any offensive way in me, and lead me in the way everlasting.*
> Psalm 139:23-24

ASK FIRST...

How would my dating standards change if I decided to treat all my dates in such a way that I would be proud to introduce any of them to my future spouse?

How will I relate to this person as God's man or God's woman?

Am I for sale?

Are my standards for sale?

I'VE ALREADY BLOWN IT —NOW WHAT?

Dear Susie,

I'm a sixteen-year-old Christian girl....I always planned on waiting to have sex, but I got in with the wrong crowd and started doing some things I knew were wrong.

When my boyfriend found out I was pregnant, he dropped me like a hot potato. Please pray for me. I believe abortion is wrong, and I don't want to do more wrong on top of what I've already done, so I've decided to have the baby. I know I will have a tough road ahead of me. Will you pray for me?

Thanks,
Jackie

Then I acknowledged my sin to you and did not cover up my iniquity. I said, "I will confess my transgressions to the LORD"—and you forgave the guilt of my sin. Psalm 32:5

Susie writes:

I had never met Jackie, but I did begin praying for her. Later, I... went to visit her in the hospital. She talked about God's forgiveness and her plans to make a fresh start. As I left the hospital that day, I prayed, "Be extra close to her, Lord...and help her to continue walking with you."

Maybe you, like Jackie, have already blown it. Maybe you haven't experienced the same painful consequences she has, but you know it's time for a change. God is ready to forgive and forget. So what is your responsibility? To seek His forgiveness. And to start over—as in establishing some new dating standards.

–Susie Shellenberger, *What Hollywood Won't Tell You About Sex, Love and Dating*

"Then neither do I condemn you," Jesus declared. "Go now and leave your life of sin."
John 8:11

WHAT GOOD IS GUILT?

> If we claim to be without sin, we deceive ourselves and the truth is not in us. 1 John 1:8

Guilt is like the oil light on the instrument panel of your life. When it comes on, it's saying, "Hey, friend, check your life! You're headed for problems if you don't!" You can choose to ignore this spiritual warning light—you may even, by repeated sinning, sever the wires that connect it—but ultimately the consequences of your sin will bring your life to a screeching halt.

Tim Kimmel, *Little House on the Freeway*

One time someone asked me, "Aren't you afraid that kids will sin more if you tell them about God's complete forgiveness?"

I replied, "Of course not! When a person really understands the unconditional love of Jesus Christ, the desire for obedience will be even greater than the desire to sin." And I pray that you will believe this good news of Jesus Christ so that you will no longer be paralyzed by your guilt. The gift of forgiveness is yours for the asking. How can you pass up such an offer of love and total acceptance?

–Jim Burns, *Radical Love*

> Therefore, if anyone is in Christ, he is a new creation; the old is gone, the new has come.
> 2 Corinthians 5:17

TOTAL LOVE

STRANGERS ARE PRAYING FOR YOU

Lord, I pray for the young man who will one day marry my daughter. That he would be a man who loves You with his whole heart; that he would love You more than he loves her. Protect his heart and mind, Lord, so that he would be able to love her with a love that's pure. Remind him to pursue You above all else. Place around him Christians who will not just point the way, but be the example he needs.

> He who walks with the wise grows wise, but a companion of fools suffers harm. Proverbs 13:20

And we pray this in order that you may live a life worthy of the Lord and may please him in every way: bearing fruit in every good work, growing the knowledge of God....

Colossians 1:10

I don't know who this man is, Lord, but help him this day to respect the girls in his life. Help him not to be overcome by passion for another, but to keep himself pure for his wedding night with our little girl. Bring him into her life at the right time. May their marriage be a light to all who see them together for many, many years to come. Amen.

–Susie Shellenberger and Greg Johnson, *258 Great Dates While You Wait*

IS IT WRONG TO FEEL THIS WAY?

If you are struggling with homosexual thoughts or temptations, remember that you do not have to act on these thoughts or give in to these temptations....Please understand that although God condemns the sin, He still loves you and wants to help you avoid this lifestyle.

–Jay Strack,
  The True Love Waits Bible

Do not be deceived: Neither the sexually immoral nor idolaters nor adulterers nor male prostitutes nor homosexual offenders nor thieves nor the greedy nor drunkards nor slanderers nor swindlers will inherit the kingdom of God. And that is what some of you were. But you were washed, you were sanctified, you were justified in the name of the Lord Jesus Christ and by the Spirit of our God. 1 Corinthians 6:9-11

No temptation has seized you except what is common to man. And God is faithful; he will not let you be tempted beyond what you can bear. But when you are tempted, he will also provide a way out so that you can stand up under it. 1 Corinthians 10:13

Homosexuality is more a matter of what you do than it is a matter of what you are.

–Greg Speck,
  Sex: It's Worth Waiting For

You cannot choose your desires, but you can choose your lifestyle.

–Tim Stafford,
  Love, Sex and the Whole Person

THE CHOICE

...AND FROM THE EXPERTS

A great many young people who come into the office these days are definitely doing it more and enjoying it less.

–Donald Holmes, Arizona psychiatrist, quoted by Josh McDowell in *Why Wait?*

The woman Folly is loud....She says to those who lack judgment. "Stolen water is sweet; food eaten in secret is delicious!" But little do they know that the dead are there, that her guests are in the depths of the grave. Proverbs 9:13, 16-18

...AND THEY'RE NOT ALONE...

Greeley's surveys show that spouses who pray together report greater marital satisfaction than those who don't, and that frequent sex coupled with frequent prayer make for the most satisfying marriages.

—*Newsweek*

Let us behave decently, as in the daytime, not in orgies and drunkenness, not in sexual immorality and debauchery, not in dissension and jealousy. Rather, clothe yourselves with the Lord Jesus Christ, and do not think about how to gratify the desires of the sinful nature.
Romans 13:13-14

A FEW MORE GOOD QUESTIONS

If your date can't respect your standards now, do you really think he or she will respect the little things that are important to you after you're married?

How could you be bound together for the rest of your life with a person who doesn't understand what it means for Christ to be the center of your life?

If someone looked at your behavior on a date, would they be able to tell that Christ is at the center of your life?

> "Blessed are those who hunger and thirst for righteousness, for they will be filled."
> Matthew 5:6

CHECK THE STATS

According to the best recent research, *Sex and the American Teenager* from Rolling Stone Press, about half of all teenagers, both male and female, stay virgins through their teenage years. I'm not denying that a lot of sexual activity goes on in high school. I know there's plenty. But there's quite a lot of determined virginity too.

–Tim Stafford, *Worth the Wait*

The most recent compilation of data from *Who's Who Among American High School Students* confirmed: In 1971, 29% of *Who's Who* students had had sex compared to 22% in 1995.

–*Youthworker Update*

> Dear friends, I urge you, as aliens and strangers in the world, to abstain from sinful desires, which war against your soul. Live such good lives among the pagans that, though they accuse you of doing wrong, they may see your good deeds and glorify God on the day he visits us.
> 1 Peter 2:11-12

THE DOUBLE-DOG-DARE

> For lack of guidance a nation falls, but many advisers make victory sure. Proverbs 11:14

This one's gonna be a stretch for you—a big stretch. In fact, I dare you, I double-dog-dare you, I triple-dog-dare you to write down any three questions about sex and go ask your parents your questions. Just think what a reaction you'll get from your friends when they ask you on the way to school what you did last night. "Oh, I had three really important questions about sex that I was dying to talk to my folks about. We ended up talking for over an hour. What did you do?"

–Joey O'Conner,
You're Grounded for Life

THE GREATEST LOVE STORIES

I know some muddle-headed Christians have talked as if Christianity thought that sex or the body, or pleasure, were bad in themselves. But they are wrong. Christianity is almost the only one of the great religions which thoroughly approves of the body—that believes that matter is good, that God himself once took on a human body....Christianity has glorified marriage more than any other religion: and nearly all the greatest love poetry in the world has been produced by Christians.

—C. S. Lewis, *Mere Christianity*

> "The thief comes only to steal and kill and destroy; I came that they might have life, and have it to the full."
> John 10:10

PORNOGRAPHY: A VICTIMLESS CRIME?

I've met a lot of men who were motivated to commit violence just like me. And without exception, every one of them was deeply involved in pornography—without question, without exception—deeply influenced and consumed by an addiction to pornography. There's no question about it...what scares and appalls me...is when I see what's on cable TV, some of the movies, some of the violence in the movies that comes into homes today was stuff that they wouldn't show in X-rated adult theaters 30 years ago.

–Ted Bundy interview with James Dobson, January 23, 1989, one day before his execution

We demolish arguments and every pretension that sets itself up against the knowledge of God, and we take captive every thought to make it obedient to Christ.
2 Corinthians 10:5

ONLY IN REAL LIFE

No one on television pays the price of illicit sex. You only do that in real life.

–Josh McDowell, *Why Wait?*

Flee from sexual immorality. All other sins a man commits are outside his body, but he who sins sexually sins against his own body.
1 Corinthians 6:18

WHAT?!

In a classic study at UCLA, 51% of male sophomores said they would rape a woman if they knew they would never get caught....[And] consider the results of a survey conducted in 1988 by the Rhode Island Rape Crisis Center...65% of the boys and 47% of the girls in seventh through ninth grades said it was okay for a man to force a woman to have sex with him if they had dated for six months or longer.

–James Dobson and Gary Bauer,
  Children at Risk

"But if anyone causes one of these little ones who believe in me to sin, it would be better for him to have a large millstone hung around his neck and to be drowned in the depths of the sea."
Matthew 18:6

WHO NEEDS ABSTINENCE?

Women of all races and ages are asking that a moral voice be heard and applauded in America. Disciplines such as abstinence yield character, self-esteem and integrity.

—Becky Tirabassi, *Being a Wild, Wonderful Woman of God*

For God did not give us a spirit of timidity, but a spirit of power, of love and of self-discipline.

2 Timothy 1:7

Today in the United States, a teenage girl gets pregnant every 30 seconds; every 11 seconds a teen acquires a sexually transmitted disease.

–Dr. Joyce Brothers,
  How to Talk with Your Kids about Sex

Do not be deceived: God cannot be mocked. A man reaps what he sows.
Galatians 6:7

AND THEY ALL SAID, "IT WON'T HAPPEN TO ME."

Do not conform any longer to the pattern of this world, but be transformed by the renewing of your mind. Then you will be able to test and approve what God's will is—his good, pleasing and perfect will. Romans 12:2

81% of sexually active girls and 60% of sexually active boys wish they had waited to have sex.

–A survey conducted by *Seventeen Magazine* and the Ms. Foundation for Women

Do you want a dating life you won't regret?

Then be the one who is setting the pace by committing from this day forward to date differently from the rest.

–Susie Shellenberger and Greg Johnson, *258 Great Dates While You Wait*

One evening a woman was driving home when she noticed a huge truck behind her that was driving uncomfortably close. She stepped on the gas to gain some distance from the truck, but when she sped up, the truck did too. The faster she drove, the faster the truck did.

Now scared, she exited the freeway. But the truck stayed with her. The woman turned up a main street, hoping to lose her pursuer in traffic. But the truck ran a red light and continued the chase.

COULD YOU BE RUNNING?

"For I know the plans I have for you," declares the Lord, "plans to prosper you and not to harm you, plans to give you hope and a future." Jeremiah 29:11

Reaching the point of panic, the woman whipped her car into a service station and bolted out of her car screaming for help. The truck driver sprang from his truck and ran toward her car. Yanking the back door open, the driver pulled out a man hidden in the back seat.

The woman was running from the wrong person. From his high vantage point, the truck driver had spotted a would-be rapist in the woman's car. The chase was not his effort to harm her, but to save her, even at the cost of his own safety.

Likewise, many people run from God, fearing what He might do to them. But his plans are for good not evil—to rescue us from the hidden sins that endanger our lives.

–Michael J. Petri, *Leadership Journal*

But Jonah ran away from the LORD.... After paying the fare, he went aboard and sailed for Tarshish to flee from the LORD. Jonah 1:3

TRUE FREEDOM

Freedom is not doing everything
you feel like doing when you feel
like doing it. Freedom is choosing
today what will give you more of
what you want tomorrow.

–Mark DeVries

Let us not become weary in doing good, for at the proper time we will reap a harvest if we do not give up. Galatians 6:9

HOW DO I START OVER?

I do not think that all who choose wrong roads perish; but their rescue consists in being put back on the right road. A wrong sum can be put right: but only by going back till you find the error and working it afresh from that point, never simply by going on. Evil can be undone, but it cannot "develop" into good. Time does not heal it. The spell must be unwound, bit by bit, "with backward musters of dissevering power"–or else not. It is still "either-or." If we insist on keeping Hell (or even earth) we shall not see Heaven: if we accept Heaven we shall not be able to retain even the smallest and most intimate souvenirs of Hell.

–C. S. Lewis, *The Great Divorce*

IN EVERY THING

> "See, I am doing a new thing!"
> Isaiah 43:19

The Holy Spirit is determined that we shall realize Jesus Christ in every domain of life, and He will bring us back to the same point again and again until we do.

–Oswald Chambers,
  My Utmost for His Highest